D0946018

KINGDOM COME

Copyright © 2011 by John Estes

All rights reserved

Printed in the United States of America

First Edition

No part of this book may be reproduced or used in any form or by any means without written permission from the publisher. This is a work of poetry; any resemblance to actual persons or events is purely coincidental. No animals were harmed.

ISBN 10: 1-936196-02-6
ISBN 13: 978-1-936196-02-9

C&R Press
812 Westwood Ave. Suite D
Chattanooga, TN 37405

www.crpress.org

Front Cover: *Aspen Stand*, by Ted Stump

KINGDOM COME

John Estes

[signature: John Est...]

[handwritten inscription:]

To Randi —
I know that you know as well as I know
that I am only guessing, + that is? much
comfort to me. As we say around our house:
you are brave + strong + true
+ may it increase. I know
that God is with you.

CONTENTS

INTERLUDE: HOME *Cosmographies*

4. IN WHICH *they seek the measure of art and love*

ACKNOWLEDGMENTS

I am grateful to the journals in which some of these poems have appeared:

ABZ, AGNI, American Poetry Journal, Another Chicago Magazine, BarfBlog, BlazeVox, Caesura, Chaffin Journal, Confrontation, Cooweescoowee, Copper Nickel, DIAGRAM, Dos Passos Review, Fox Cry Review, Front Porch Journal, GW Review, A Handsome Journal, If, inscape, Jellyroll, Kansas English, LIT, Literary Imagination, The Literary Review, Makeout Creek, MARGIE, Mochila Review, Ninth Letter, New Delta Review, New Orleans Review, Not Just Air, Notre Dame Review, Packingtown Review, Permafrost, Plains Song Review, Poetry Daily, Portland Review, Red Mountain Review, Southern Review, Terrain.org, Tin House, Tusculum Review, Two Hawks Quarterly, Wallace Stevens Journal, West Branch, and *Verse Daily.*

To the Poetry Society of America and C. K. Williams for a National Chapbook Fellowship and the publication of *Swerve* (2009), in which some of these poems appear.

To Carol Muske-Dukes for her first belief, and all my teachers.

And to those who have sheltered me.

for Jennifer Ruth

In love all that counts is the act.
—*August Rodin*

He takes from his fields and from his orchard boughs
What they have offered of their own free will.
—*Virgil*, Georgics

I do not know what is untried and afterward,
But I know it is sure and alive, and sufficient.
—*Walt Whitman*

Emptied Term

Poets behave ruthlessly
toward their own experiences: they exploit them.
—*Friedrich Nietzsche*

The day the spotting stopped
being spots it rained all day.

What drove the weather-beaten
carcass of a squirrel
to come down
from the old tree nest
on that of all rainy days
I couldn't guess,
but while hardly a haruspex
the pit in my gut understood that

—if what originates springs—

our is, our might-have-human-been
was not to be

and in that heart-sunk instant knew
this visitation was not news to be reported.

Though my backyard sorrow paled
beside her indoor grief,

the tremble of shame was mine alone:
dread of the miscarriage poem

that might be avoided
but would not be averted.

CHAPTER 1

IN WHICH *love and art seek their measure*

By intuition alone can man love and know either woman
or the world, and by intuition alone can he bring forth
again images of magic awareness which we call art.

—*D. H. Lawrence*

The Eternal Body of Man Is the Imagination

> Paradise. The course of a boat.
> Relations between a man and a woman.
> —"Things That Are Near Though Distant"
> *The Pillow Book of Sei Shonagon*

This gospel of loneliness
says two pleasures endure:
those of the flesh
and those of the writing table.

Once—I remember it
clearly being the eighth day
of the twelfth month;
the moon had brightened
in the heavy air,
and the paper birch
outside my apartment door
the kids had stripped
until nearly bare,
littering its bed
with twists of bark—
I had a vision,
an insight so stark
and lucid I knew it must
be heeded, the kind
one typically
must fast to receive
or live up a tree for weeks
to call down from the heavens
or up from animals.
I was in love, terrified.

And as the text says:
the mind is never at ease
upon Osaka's slope.

It went down like this:
as she exited the shower,
grabbed her towel,
I felt—not a voice,
not a flash or the quivering
fade-out movies
contrive to such effect—
but a swift severing,
like the strike of a blade;
my mindeye snatched a glint
of the samurai *katana,*
surely wielded (I later divined)
by a gaunt legislator/
priest of the not-so-holy invisible.
It cleaved—God
what a woman, what a gift—
the steamy air and laid
open the dilemma:
some men are bound
to the misery of a single pleasure,
others to a misery
of not knowing
which pleasure is theirs.

Our pact, a kind *amor fati*
and Rilkean math,
carried over its unimagined

pain to deviations
all too non-imaginary:
splitting griefs,
guilt for undone acts, chances
left with chance.
Who, at last, will care
if I forsake the pine trees,
the wisteria,
or the yellow roses?
If I choose dumplings
over the cherry blossoms?
In what equation
is sacrifice either square or root?

On Flight 898 to New York, via Atlanta

It is not today as O'Keeffe painted it—
     mackerel sky of billow-snippet clouds
far into the horizon.
         Still, exhausted with awe.
Closing the shade I wonder: where in this world
     is so much plastic molded?

It's snowing, huge impulsive gusts.
    Before we could fly they had to neutralize
      the snow (aka "the contaminant")
with peachy goo shot from a fire hose.

Amidst boot camp recruits
    on edge and en route to Ft. Jackson,
kids who've never flown, much
       less left the farm or killed a man,
    I keep jolting awake
     as if nodding off at the wheel.

It is not at all as O'Keeffe saw it—
    happy blue field of cuckoo altocumulus.
No apparent sun in the sky above,
the cloud cover is thick and vast and gray so that
     breaking through it
      a man thinks
he could swim in it, craves to—
    if not for the deterrent threat
  of affection
    a man might build a nest to contain—
if not for this percussion glass.

A Kind of Retinal Registration

> The best drama is one that deals with a man in danger.
> —*Howard Hawks*

He asked if she caught ever out the corner
of her periphery a shape
or motion the mind
configured as a person or (as it must) a phantom

Months pass and no theatrical answer
can out-climax
remembering the presence
of a question
now that the affair's idea had so far entered
the body
it became his body
so eviscerated by secrets no
right-minded ghost would dare inhabit it

Answers are denouement
she might have said
if she talked like that instead of
thought like that
until it was clear to her
how a character inclined to dissolution
finds dissolution and sought-for
specters of peripety
unknot problems only they can create
and on her mark
she said yes

It was the looked-for sign of arriving love
a looked-for kind of lie

Theological Doubt of the French Symbolists

So: you've given up on correspondence
and now talk on the phone instead.

The other day you finally made sense
when you said,
        "A tree's a tree; now let's go to bed."

Have you ever seen the sun alight
upon a spray? A single branch, spread
up and up and then—*chosen*?
        How might we mince

words no longer? How might we apply
the opening of our ends?

Let's go ahead: no matter the stylus, no
matter the wax,
        a mark's a mark and will be read.

St. Francis Reads *The Kama Sutra*

The dead are not so easily de-educated—
    several ways have been tried
to reform, to shift a habit
into a memory and back again: implants
                and transplants and all artificial
means of arousal fail from these locations.

Sexual relations can be diversified by studying
    the habits of animals, domestic and wild,
           and even insects.

It's as though, three-quarters naked already,
    as if in getting back to nature they—
well, we—believed you when you told us to seek
original mind below, or within,
      or above, as if a lover,
        like all deep bass sounds, weren't nondirectional.

Rooster Rock

When the eye sees beauty, the hand wants to draw it.
—*Ludwig Wittgenstein*

What happened,
what impulse did I obey,
at the top
of that monument,
that rock, that moved
me to spill
my seed, to call
from depths
like a kraken of joy
my weedy salt?
Poor, unsuspecting
slug at my boots—
poor cloud-broke sky—
assaulted by
the yawp of Onan.

Oregon woods,
wet, steep, and overrun,
guilty with moss
and rhododendrons—
Sorry: I left a trace.
Though far, far
from any place or
one I know,
I mourn, in secret,
our lost days
and crossed stars.
Who can say
what creatures,
if happy, we'd become?

State of the Art

A poem in Sioux Falls, itself once saved
    like this, talked a jumper down.
A poem takes you by the hand, compliments
    your shoes, makes you ask for its number.
Poems love attention and little gifts, but many
    thrive on abuse. Go ahead—try it!
Some poem or other no doubt tried to make
    a move on your high school boyfriend.
    He let it, and that's where he learned
    to do that thing.
Poems make good chains, garage rags,
    and in some cultures palate cleansers.
My cousin had a poem once that always tried
    to hump the leg of house guests.
You know those disorienting moments
    when you think you saw this moment
    in a dream? That's a poem.
Five or more poems hanging out, wearing
    similar colors—move quickly and quietly
    to the other side of the street.
Never attempt to save a drowning poem
    by swimming to it.
Red sky at night, poem's delight; red sky
    at morning—poems don't give a shit.
    They sleep in.
Kissing your sister is, by definition, a poem.
In some areas, poem populations are reaching
    nuisance levels. Agencies have reintroduced
    natural predators; qualified hunters
    have been allotted increased bag limits.

Most poems were obsessive masturbators
        when young, and swore they'd stop when
        or before they became adults.
Quality spare parts for poems can be hard to find.
Poems and elbows are safe to put in your ear.
Stacked atop each other, poems make nice
        monuments; skillfully arranged in a circle,
        stood on end, you've got a nifty hovel
        for your garden gnome.
I suspect the Batboy of being a poem.
Poems have learned the hard way to keep
        their politics to themselves, but a few
        drinks will often open them up.
Whatever Jesus wrote in the dirt, with his
        finger, that's the ur-poem.
Sometimes, because they like irony, poems
        wear suits and work as business-types.
Lacking couth as well as loving comfort,
        even these poems rarely wear underwear.
Most drug stores carry poem masks year-round.
Some poems sing quite well, but the wise
        remain wary of falling in love with them
        on that account.
Poems are chronically susceptible to liver
        and foot disorders; many wear glasses.
Too much blue eye shadow is a guilty
        pleasure for many poems.
Next Christmas, donate to your favorite poem
        on behalf of a loved one or friend.
Experience shows poems make better lovers
        than spouses. There are exceptions.

The Male Gaze (Ending with a Sentence by Frank Bidart)

If it's true, as Longfellow said,

      that a man must be either anvil

or hammer,

          too much remains unseen to say

what a woman is,

      or a beloved,

      or even the object—

agent, actor, act,

the scene itself unfolding

      toward catastrophe—or if this is all

         as bad as it sounds: to be rapt,

or objectified,

      or if bringing back is the action

         that connects us

    to what, together, we perform.

And of course it's not true.

Forgive me my unchaste eye.

         I'd ask to be

unfastened from

    this tyranny of relation, but

   care of the body is referred (if any)

      to the soul.

We fill pre-existing forms, and when we fill them, change them

    and are changed.

D. H. Lawrence, Painter

For $2 paid to New Mexico's last living
witness to his town square
wife beatings
(she works behind the desk of the Hotel La Fonda in Taos
and will reluctantly chronicle
Lorenzo's pale-faced rages,
how he'd knock
Frieda in the dirt for smoking)
admission to his gallery
and the unexpurgated privilege
of ruminating
on canvas after canvas of
plump asses
fat and loafy
body upon body
upon trees upon beasts
the realism of a father's brown hand pressed
against a wife's fleshy breast
as a child sits at breakfast
      looking blithely on
is mine.

Whether artistic merit (as such)
can transfigure
the goatish phantasia
of nuns stumbling upon a naked man
sleeping beneath a tree
his penis a drooped swart radish
or invest with social good
a man pissing into a dandelion patch
or a swan mounting a most-willing Leda
or justify
whatever that phallic obelisk
prominent on a high hill
stands to declare

about the spirit-engrossed
the corrupt and blessedly-so nature
of erotic encounters
        remains the bright particular corpse
the exhibit proposes to buy.

All of which depends on whether
sheer sensuality purifies (as he says)
and quickens the mind
or whether art
(or whatever he means by the root
and quick of his darkness)
is in fact the real enigma.
When any curved line can suggest the feminine principle
bending prosaically toward rebirth
when endless circle after circle of holy disgust
sputters to a halt
at the horny feet of biography
we fumble
        relativists in search of the original cold black state
backward toward resolution—

As a matter of conscience
Frieda would rage
        and find strange men to bang and with vengeance
be made whole.

CHAPTER 2

IN WHICH *he marries*

The purpose of marriage is to teach a man to be
happy with one woman.

—*St. John Chrysostom*

Epithalamium

Nothing says I love you
    like a borehole will. A trepanned skull,
like an eye emptied
      of intention—lazy how
    a lion is lazy—draws out or lulls scattering
phantasms to abandon
    their nests, our earthly wounds.

You can see now how the blind spot
    got built in, not yet
      selected against,
and perhaps more easily accept the junction
    of gaps—however acute
      but coarse the image—that presents itself,
easy as anesthesia, like signing the release
    or convalescence or
      taking to auger against doctor's orders,
a cold compress holding
    the stitches in where your nevermore
      once dwelled.

The chamber cleared,
    garments cleaned and ready,
    no force can welcome duty's threshold
like the common picture
    of a hollow cup:

a ganglion want
    is made worthy by a sharp lookout
    and a nerve for it.

Purpose-built from Household Objects

Being a good boy, he traded
in (believing
he traded up) his being
for meaning
as it is said all men must do,
but he's neglected, unread,
the fine print terms of its warranty.
Buried in a disheveled
stack on a bottom shelf
with other guides and manuals,
it awaits a breaking
to need fixed.

Not coincidentally, the timing
coincided with realizing:
a woman, unlike space- or labor-
saving appliances,
might help him
deliver more than promise,
produce more than consume;
that his brain may be less
Cuisinart/Jenn-Air
than a secondhand stamped-blade
butcher's knife
thrown in for free with a stump-legged
butcher's block;
that while it may be true
that What We See is What We Think—
as his insurance agent taught him—
and correct to say
the good man has no shape,

it may not always be the case
that the rock, like the man, is but an icon.

Sure, he misses the old days,
the breathing-
and prayer-without-ceasing,
the unaccountable infinity of laundry
that never congregates in piles.
The reverie benders,
the indolent pleasure of starts
without finishes.
An entire life devised as groundwork.
Simply to own a rake
did the trick and the neighbors
supplied first aid
and Sunday evening dinners.
Now that his hungers
are mingled with and no
longer mingling,
and longing is synonymous
with shopping;
now when the hulking, arrhythmic
refrigerator/freezer
rattles as it cycles down
and its gray-noise motor hum
is noticed:
silence is finally defined.

The Marriage Bed

> If the bee disappeared off the surface of the earth,
> man would have no more than four years to live.
> —*Albert Einstein*

First, there's the guilt—at least
for those who grew up
hooked on *Little House on the Prairie*,
watching Pa tenderly
cobble Ma a hickory-log frame
for her hand-sewn mattress
stuffed with shrub grass,
or those who cannot undiscover
the moment of unfolding
in Homer's *Odyssey*,
where Odysseus passes
crafty Penelope's identity test
by describing, with meticulous detail,
how he built their bedroom
around the four-poster
hand-hewn from a rooted olive tree—
the signature guilt
of buying one's marriage bed
off a showroom floor.

In the *Georgics* Virgil describes
how if one's honeybee hive—
Latin *cubile*, the same word used
for the bridal chamber
couch Tithonos and Aurora share
each night before she,
replenished, arises
at dawn to don her saffron robes—

goes dead and silent
one can call them back to existence.
Whether killed off cursed
by nymphs or mutant fungus
or just bad luck, despite the alert
protections of Priapus,
one must sacrifice a young bullock.
Stuff its orifices with marjoram
and thyme, beat its bones
and innards soft then let it rot
in a closed-up hut
with four small windows.
Then, after a hot and windy
season, *mirabile dictu*: this fermenting
viscera will burst forth
a buzzing, nectar-sucking swarm.

Then, there's the rift—
though we agree that any debt
is better than sleeping
ensconced in the cheap veneer
of Mexican-made consumer goods—
the signal rift
between what we say,
what we are,
and what we recognize as so.
Am I a giant-eyed drone?
Are you an egg-rich queen?
Are we no more than common
workers, bees
of an easily blighted invisible?

The Existence of the World Is a Controversy

After the photograph, the class wandered
off and I wondered why so often I found myself
the last man. Because I'd read Emerson
all summer long, I took my lack
of discomfort to be a sign of heroic standing.

So I determined to set for myself a new relation
to the universe, to write poems.
As if one could settle, once and for all, the question
whether or not vocation is all.

Solitude can become a rotten habit.
I remember how acute the contentment,
Friday nights especially, my reflection in the television.

What passes for turning inward, for study and for art,
can slip unnoticed into a well-practiced jeopardy,
a narrative fortress projecting the story
of separation into a post-quotidian SIGNIFICANT LIFE.
A myth is a lie breathed through silver.

Peace, not necessarily the doing of peaceful spirits,
can lead to believing that being a person is easy.

On my honeymoon, I thought to myself
You'll never be alone again. Inside
the wigwam suite, clothes scattered
around the bearskin rug, an Indian-warrior
gelatin print—his feathers new, his face
deep-lined and droughted—as my eyewitness,
I wondered what might happen
if I surrendered, with a few conditions,
to this bright casualty.

Symptomatic, Asymptotic

Comes up somewhere   shy
of pastoral, bucolic.
Not quite a green thought—
40% chance turned
downpour—but greening,
a farmable (read firm,
read pharmaceutic) mutation:
sheep beget a shepherd,
beget the shepherdess beget
the sheepfold beget
begetting and bleating need
for the arable, the potable,
the strip mall, the big
box and a blockbuster ethos.
From the flood
of plastic entertainments,
a short leap to the purple pill.

The hole in the forest
they dug and stuck
our house in after they cut
the trees out fills
with the neighbors' runoff;
sewerworks are a miracle,
working or not.
You emerge from
the mudroom, the laundry
done and lovely,
tell me the drain is clogged
but surely know better

than I—desuetude
where duende
is needed—what Hölderlin
meant when he said
a life, if poetic, measures
and dwells.

Tuesday, plying my
elevation trade I told them:
at the end, never locate
your epiphany in—
or else approach only
rarely and with care
(if locate one you must)—
water, light,
fire, moon and stars,
especially wings,

hands. They added   rain.

The Narcissism of Minor Difference

> ...each unhappy family is unhappy in its own way.
> —*Leo Tolstoy*

The Karenina Principle states:
        an error
in one strain
        of a multi-variable system
                dooms the system.

Thus a happy family,
        like any contrivance
                that works,
        hinges on, depends upon,
        anomaly—
random statistical variation
        held together
                by the duct tape of duty
and the floss of luck.

Some accidents
        are less accident
        than languid probability,
scavenging for food and struggling
        to cross the tracks.
Thus the cowcatcher.

Although we took no vows,
        made no public promises,
        we practice our perfection
the way a buzzard,
        when it believes no one listens,

will crash through branches
                    and attack, attack, attack—
then circle
         for a time
the carcass it made
         before descending on its appetite.
           This reassures the order
that what the order assumes
                  it assumes.

         Nothing has changed,
      but oh what a nothing.

CSI: Where It's Remembered That the Phoenix and the Turtledove Died of Married Chastity in Shakespeare's Long-lost Poem

After days of trace analysis on what ails us—fibers resembling your
        shirt fibers
delicately collected, prints resembling my boot prints
lifted from the ground of angered exegesis—still, the scene is littered,
circumstantially, with evidence of love's blunt trauma.

Ballistics is stumped: no verified match, only cautious conclusions:
"indications point, "origins suggest," "within statistical margins
        of probability."

———————————

If the want of hospitality makes any place a hospital—
just as the gross weight of humility,
rightly figured, is a constituent of humiliation—
we're lucky:
weight is a force, force times distance traveled is work,
and work beats the wrench out of heartache.

But the energy contained in any object at any instant is constant
(in the absence of constant motion),
so that must be how the mythic lovers scorched each other
        inscrutable, to ashes,
exhausting the laws of conservation
until only birds, dead, remain, though they do sigh.

A List of What Is Found

> How the state is to be made safe from cows
> is a saga yet to be written.
> —*Aldo Leopold*

The old Burlington
Northern rail bed touches
the southern edge
of the yard
not a hundred feet
from where we're staying—
a ghostly, trackless
river of gray gravel
embowered by cottonwood
and hedge, thickened
with pines and red cedar.
Our hosts tell us—
as two wrens zip around
rebuilding their
poorly placed
nest the Doberman
ate babies-and-all—
how an easterly wind would
blow the approaching
rumble off and so a throbbing
hulk of diesel engine
towing 100+ coal cars
could suddenly darken
their back deck,
a paracletic comfort
(in retrospect, at least)
abandoned for a bike trail.

I've come to Kansas
to do a job,

to inventory a store of books—
the endangered kind
housed in old Victorians
where light switches
hide behind Kierkegaard
and the bathroom is
a stockroom stockpiling
stacks of bargain-buy lectures
on Aquinas on Aristotle,
titles they account for
in years per turn
not turns per year—
which means forsaking books
to better address
the shelf-worn menace
of our bourgeois
contentment.
An old copy of Thoreau
sits on the stand
calling out alongside
other diluted (i.e., textual)
libidinal oppositions:
bloodless
and rational words
of institution
that mock a project's
scope and scale
but safeguard a life,
so designed, of convention.

On the news:
in the desert outskirts
of an Iraqi town,
the so-called Triangle of Death,

a patrol is ambushed:
five dead—
3389, 3390, 3391, 3392, 3393—
three unaccounted for.
Our host descends
to remind us over 3000 die
worldwide each day
in car crashes.

High Fidelity

Bored by an intifada
too easily won, the evil one—
cross-dressed for success
in a moleskin cassock,
skullcap and cowl—
with cheap theatrics
fashions out of immanence
all imaginable acts,
overturning the precedence
of adulterous miseries.
Physicists call it
action-at-a-distance,
where *momentaneous*
is a slick synonym
for *speed of light*.
For this reason occult
gurus who slept in caves
but feared sleep
said thoughts must
be murdered before they can
penetrate the heart's
soft-tissued penetralium.

To catch, not to mention kill
(not to mention not
be killed by)
a motion of the mind
requires what ocularists,
with envy,
know as *smooth pursuit*:

that tracking function
perfected by our meat-stalking
forebears, the want
for which explains why
the glass-eyed kid in gym
class sat out kick-
and dodge- and softball.

The bodhisattvas say
the way past undue love
(meaning any love)
is to envision women
(or what-have-you)
as sacks of guts, given to rot.
O my love, my love,
I am doomed
by your beautiful viscera.

No Man's Land

There's nothing discordant in wanting

I have to keep telling her that

See how the hard freeze roughs the rosemary up

Burns the more fragile searchlight arcs

Of twisted thyme and the fountainous sage

Spreading across and down the stone retaining wall

See what you've been spared

My god if only the sparing ever stopped

But it doesn't even care to stop

It evades my barbed wire perimeter

The towers and Mauser-armed guards

The wrangling distractions and the lone resistant

Strain of opening space

Infinitely small infernally spacious

She says I'd get farther faster if my art

Were inflected or twinged with the requisite

Grief but really I'm not sad

Marriage, in absentia

The blank tile toils to represent.
        A blank, like all vacua, stands for itself
    and everything possible,
                counters the music it courts
      without limit,
           with a value of exactly zero.

Aristotle said friends are not friends
             unless they share life in common,
because friendship is an act,
      not a state,
               and time gives it proof
in the only way time evinces anything,
    in waiting, in the *passio* of turn-taking games.

When you return, we will resume it.

To live in mortal fear
         of one's capacity for betrayal,
    as I do,
                is not quite what the mythos
means when it praises
      fear as sacred wisdom.
    There is little honor in saving one's skin by violence,
      and according to half-world lore
            only the trace residue of pliant forces—
        like the garden slug's silvery contrail-slime
or the earthy smell of children
          after playing outdoors—
can put down the serpent and the wolf.

No faith survives without a dragon's sleep,
                without the antonym of one-eyed discipline.
If evil exists, it's defined as that which has no end.

Note Proposition 11, *Guide for the Perplexed*:
        "The existence of the infinite is in every respect impossible."

This sentence is based on the reasonable belief
                that motion cannot endure,
                        that succession cannot be ensured ad infinitum.

Desires this precise, this surgical,
        render moot the question of more or less deceived.

The pause speaks on behalf of the stop,
                and serves as the pit around which I gather
            and talk as if rehashing
                        a favorite self-judgment
                    or encomium to all things wild and free.

I've heard it said the purpose of marriage,
                in essence, is solace:
                        a tithe to need I once called weakness.
        I'm still skeptical,
but I can embrace the solace of ideas,
        and so even the idea of you,
                like the idea of clearing one's letter rack,
can keep me on pace,
                        stretched out toward the thing itself
                despite an excessive run of vowels
        or the smolder one marries to contain.

What I would give for the company of a hawk or heron—
        or even a river, where the kingfisher

comes to hover and hunt.
Somewhere to go for my totems to be replenished.

Our house, even empty, remains a shelter,
       a lean-to sufficient for refuge that spares me
              from turns I could not withdraw.

The porch light just came on.
Its motion sensor is misgauged, and case-sensitive.
Maybe a possum, maybe a passing car.
       But this will serve for the green beacon.
       This will do for a sign: the way back has been barred.

DECIMATE is what I can muster—for now, for 13 points—
                       a wasted blank.

Sufficient Wildness

> The seeds of instinct are preserved under the thick hides
> of cattle and horses, like seeds in the bowels
> of the earth, an indefinite period.
> —*Henry David Thoreau*

Nickel or dime
me each time
love needed rope
or explosives
to sprout—
bloom, blossom,
whatever
one calls the stage
one stops
to note how bodies
wring or erupt
into colors—
and I'd be rich.

The beholder,
I know. I confess
a despotic eye,
a tyrannical initial
disposition.
Who couldn't guess
that, though?
It's not news
to say the passions
ascend/descend
the throne of
every fiefdom.
News me about
the fief.

Wednesday last
I read in *Walden:*
"The civilized man is a more experienced
 and wiser savage."
My wife and I
argued, our regularly
scheduled domestic
disturbance
to fix the terms
of home
and art repair.
Not exactly Peter
robbing Paul,
but same synagogue.
The dogs
dug under
and escaped the fence.
We concluded
that like trees
our virtues, if any,
lie in being
unable to be
otherwise. But
even a thief must
be sheltered.

That love is
a daemon or that
backyard grass
will not revive
I readily concede.
What resists
by enchantment
or graft its
own transformation

the chemists
and spendthrifts and I
agree is devilish.
But wrath, as
in Woden's wrath,
as in a fury
furious enough to pluck
out its own eye
for the sake of poetry—
that travels best
in countries
where love goes
for what maims you.
I skip the God-
term on purpose;
what I plant
each year, manure
but never water
never fails, as yet,
to yield.

CHAPTER 3

IN WHICH *a child is conceived and born*

To the Greeks *tekhne* means neither art nor handicraft but rather: to make something appear, within what is present, as this or that, in this way or that way.

—*Martin Heidegger*

Essay on Baby-making

> She wraps them in a strange garment of flesh.
> —*Empedocles*

It *is* merciless
to conjure a life
onto a leaden,
particulate-laden
molten rock,
though once here
sorrow struggles
to obtain; even
the suicide
has brooded on
love enough
to name it cruel—
albeit dull
and granulated,
overwhelming
with novelty—
by the time
the final
inventory is taken.

The terrorist,
like any professional,
grounds his fear
in reverence.

The viburnum
is in bud; the toaster

is mysteriously
set to Dark
each morning;
my uncle's
prostate, mission
accomplished,
metastasizes
and here we are,
brightening
the red sauce
with fresh basil,
breeders—
and not sorry.

School of Prophets

Cursed be the man before the Lord that riseth up and
buildeth this city Jericho: he shall lay the foundation in his firstborn,
and in his youngest shall he set up the gates of it.
—*Joshua 6:26*

Standing at the center urinal
waiting on the urine,
I saw, with the prescience
of Elijah, a scene
as sure to come to pass
as the piss I coaxed: me, the same
but maybe waiting longer
with my sons on either side,
spraying our cakes
with readymade fountains.
I will have trained them
not to be omphaloskeptic types
who stare at their hands
throughout the maneuver,
but rather to handle each crisis
with sprezzaturic ease,
the crack finesse
of an artist adept at hiding his art.

I feel, even now—sensing
them, their sideways
glances—no small surge of pride
in this feat, at the double
portion of my spirit
split and shared,
unequal but without enmity.

Once the fiery chariot,
complete with fiery horses,
lifts me in the whirlwind
never to return,
they will at least have that:
a kind of mantle
and a bone-rattling faith
with which
to smite the waters of Jericho
and later heal them.

Mating Rituals of the Doctor of Philosophy

In my latest theory of appearing
I contest the equation
that putting oneself to bed
measures some essence
of maturity or that a nursery
is where babies sleep,
not where babies get made.

Though I hazard to guess
that in our economy
where being-at-work is
ennobled when we
(in our proletarian way)
call love what Aristotle called
being-at-work-staying-itself,
we fool ourselves
to believe in our own potential,
to insist, as we do,
on the existence of a given
that nonetheless needs us.

Still, I will sire no tribe of fops
between our sheets
between the hours of 10 and 6.

We drink to the world as unfinished,
but do not drain our glasses.

To My Sperm, Nightswimming

Off she goes, and you with her—
"Verticality is your worst
enemy" were my last words—to bed,
to sleep, perchance to conceive.
Godspeed your ploughs, my friends,
uphill through the gannet's bath,
meniscus-smeared in porpoise
oil to protect against the elements.

Our fate, my ardent if ambivalent
desire for abundance, I entrust
to some one of you: handless hands,
super-conducive high-capacity
noggin and the scourge of that killer

flagellum. Farewell to comrades
and weaker fellow travelers
who fall or falter off the beeline.

A lunatic blue lifts and springs
the tides tonight, so ride or outride
the propagating waves engined
on these mensal syzygies—gamete
earth, thanatos sun, nuciform
moon—and surge:
sea- or sky- or homeward
toward your bountiful oblivion.

Macculate Conception

No stars, no kings, no prophecies, no barren
    wombs miraculously opened, just
    the slow steady play, inning by inning
    of a disciplined defense

We wait for the waking of Brahma
    to stir against whatever the neighbors bang on
    to shake off the worlds that passed
    themselves for dreams, to stumble in his midnight
    naked for the bedside yarrow stalks
    and, later, a change of linens

We won't deny the divination or a need
    for insufficient language
    to suggest or speculate on a special
    use of the ordinary one

We shouldn't deny that somewhere
    there's a place where theories can exist
    without the burden of prediction

And a realm, at least, where the statistics
    we're amassing are more
    than trivia, more than pink streaks
    on a stick you pissed on,
    more than our need to know the meaning
    of what changes—*Thunder over Water, Earth over Wind*—
    that stain, that spotless stain

Body World(s)

> Death will return us to that condition of tranquility
> which we enjoyed before we were born.
>
> —*Seneca*

It's a bit too easy, too cute:
  the little kid, who calls the plastinated manikins naked,
      plays a game pointing out his father's nose, his ears, his mouth
  facing the annotated banner of Vesalius' Anatomy Theater,
      behind the bastardized Nietzsche quote and delineated Hamlet,
          near the display case of blackened smokers' lungs,
          next to the exploded, tripartite gymnast,

  despite the parental warnings, oblivious to his education,

oblivious to his mother, the pregnant one the teenage girls keep an eye on
who goes behind the discreet black curtain to see the fetuses.

The docent comes over, tells them in her loud whisper
  to quiet down. As if we were in the presence of the dead
      who by definition must—right?—decompose or at least decay,

          must be some fraction water to deserve our reverence.

Rumormongers say these are smuggled Chinese corpses,
      sex slaves and executions, victims of some version of a long knife.
  Ask these Körperkünstler if their body art achieves Gestalt,
                              as advertised,
          or if they've found a rift
              where love and hate and world and earth
                  no longer strive.
  Regardless of provenance or fiat these grim immortalists,
          as Tu Fu might have said, have no tea in them.

The father and his son move on and the boy
    takes interest in the flayed Skin Man, who holds aloft his epidermis
        which the kid keeps calling a popped balloon.

One only hopes the installation's thesis—
        knowledge of the flesh, even (especially) humorless flesh without
            its data, will give one peace with death—
    is lost on him.

Birth Class

When the doula—hip, Gaea-like,
bright porcelain doll (mere
birth assistant to those unstrained
by midwifery, by the magic
adjectives *natural*, *spiritual* and *vaginal*)—
asked us to write, "What
comes to mind when I say 'pregnant'
or when I say 'labor'?"
my mind of shame said WORK LIBERATES,
aping the gates of Auschwitz.

And when the striped-tie Smart Guy
said, "It has a terminus," I heard
Plath say, "Boarded the train
there's no getting off."
When the Second-Timer called it
an out-of-body experience
I'm sure, I thought, I heard a Fly buzz.

The stuffed pelvis appeared, full
of milk chocolate stuffed baby,
its snap-on umbilical cord
drawing its eggplant placenta,
and Maxine Kumin's woodchuck
presented its wily head, crowned before
showing us a cardinal turn,
its impudent art of unschooled survival.

A cesarean section she compared
to rummaging through a dresser drawer:
its glass knobs missing, I imagined.

Undone by birth films—the screams
and groans and last-pushes,
the calamities exalted
to bloody last-second elections—
I heard the psalmist
saunter through strumming,
"God is a butter mountain,"
followed by A. R. Ammons prosaically
denoting the poem a walk:
a verbal means to a non-verbal source.

The California Dude asked her
what *exactly* a contraction
does and how could I not,
as she mapped the crosshatched
striations of the common womb,
see the wreath'd trellis
of Keats' brain, that bower
of delight and shadowy thought
where a casement left ope at night
lets the warm Love in?
And how could I not transition
from the silicone breast
to breathing techniques and not,
like a stalled uterus—
as they diagnose it when a mother's
progress fails—feel eclipsed
by this weight
a woman's solstice makes?

Country Matters

Dear Vern,
Think of you often and remembering
the days long ago when we lived in Pleasant Valley.

Jess

Fished out of a ditch, in a bundle of other
      dead letters, this rip of card becomes a woman's
clever bookmark, a memento mori, a scrap now

      marking her way through *The Complete Poems*
of Elizabeth Bishop. The cursive script, shaky
      but deliberate, evokes film of an aged debutante,

hair newly coiffed, seated at a faded white,
      slightly French escritoire, the muslin-draped
room stifling with dust and rose water.

      For a long time she simply holds the pen.
Since no lady dare face, much less reveal,
      the fullness her heart imposes, she's content

to feel the traceried edge of her recollection
      as fine enough. When I find her note—it slips out
place-keeping for "Questions of Travel"—

      do I call that *sympathy,* that jolt of awakened
agony when I read her courtesy as loss?
      I'm not wrong (am I?) to hear in her nostalgia

contours of a lonely handmade cosmos,
      built to house her pains against their vanishing?
Sorry: it's hard to see beyond what is written.

Whatever kept Jess from loving Vern feels
small tonight, and their last walk,
        on which possibilities were hinted,

where tiny lies were told—when regret
        seemed spared—must be what rehearses
itself like a gift she isn't grateful for.

        Not every soul is so blessed, to be saved
from its own avid inclinations.
        When Emerson unearthed his firstborn

Waldo's rotting corpse because he longed
        to clutch him years after scarlet
fever took him, was it then he realized that sacred

        history attests the poet's birth as principal event?
Or maybe it was only then he understood
        that utterance's bitter logic. It may be true,

poets live in suspended adolescence,
        that fevers try their best to serve the creature.
But as Emerson in his floruit professed,

        taken for a fool is the territory's terrain,
a hazard of the purchase but a bargain
        at the cost. When I think of Emerson, I think

not of a new theogony, but of this twilight
        looting and—as I picture it—the shuddering
sobs ignorant of the brittle stench,

and wonder how he knew he'd had enough,
what signal told him to give the boy,
    this once bright dream, back to his trench.

Out here on the ranch, we control
    our cows by letting them graze, and rivers
carry strains of sadness so far-sourced

    from high hills it maddens the clarity
of our expecting. As Auden figured it,
    the place where beauty is just compensation

for what happens elsewhere and dinners
    are assured is called the Valley of Its Making.
Here, the spinster's art is a grave concern,

    as are soft spots that won't close. We conduct
our business, love and judge, with eyes open.
    Now that my son is on the way, the deed secured,

the neighbors keep asking if I'm excited.
    No, not exactly: this latest quill of never-agains
takes time to be made native. If resistance—

    the most pleasurable stage of separation
in this centrifuge of marriage
    and baby-making—begins to feel like bad faith,

I remember that out here on the ranch,
    where a mouth only eats what the hands
can earn it, we always need the help.

The Fish Turned Toward Shore

> The fish turned toward shore.
>
> —*Jaws*

The fish turned toward shore
    and in its fishy way: *Harrumph*. So that's the deep,
a hollow throbbing in the ear tube
and tribulating rills along the lateral line. What
    is heard, or sensed there—what others
call the deep's deep, or with a flourish the deepening deep—
    is not the place imagined but a little shift
    in pressure, a slipping out of work boots into
house shoes so far gone unshifted. Not that a fish,
any more than any creature, minds being lied to;
    not that on the belief-level of the ear stone
it didn't comprehend how, beneath the weight
of all that water, the situation couldn't help but get
    out of hand. Just that it, maybe more than
other creatures, learns by habit to trade on the side
of silence, and isn't prepared for the kind surprise
    of shallows which—maybe by its shoaling, maybe
its kelpy trusses or its equalizing zeal—cannot
help but be mistaken, on occasion, as having uttered
    Fish, turn toward the shore.

Well Begun Is Half Done

No crib, but late naps, early
    milkings and a gibbous moon,
a storm door the midwives
    broke, cold front impinging
fitful spring: each intimates
    a future repair just as this sweet
parenthesis, this sanctuary
    from the cares we thought we
lived by, closes with the advent
    of family visitations. They would
think me dark and default
    to awkward pauses, shuffling
the conversation to sleep
    and feedings, patterns of slack
advice about beginnings, if only
    they knew only now, if only briefly,
do I meet the shade of endings
    with indifference, if not scorn,
as anything but the drowsy
    unsealed sliver of some waxing
random moon.

I Foresee the Breaking of All That Is Breakable

Perhaps after all it is, merely, a desire
to use the word *thanatopsical*—
but if you can wash or handle
artifacts like this blue
tea mug, carried from Crete as a gift
from a friend, or this nacreous
orange bowl,
a honeymoon souvenir
bought in a now-defunct artists'
shop in Colorado, or
this antique Chinese mudman
carrying his sponges
and fish from a day at the pier,
without a pathological
fixation on the day you will stumble
and drop it, or smack it
against the sink divider or brush
it with a hand reaching
for the letter opener, you are *junzi*:
a superior person, as Confucius had it.
You probably make love
to your spouse without imagining
betrayal and pay taxes
without complaint
because you think nothing
in truth belongs to you.

They invented the earth for people
like you, and then salted it.

HOME *Cosmographies*

If I were asked to name the chief benefit of the house,
I should say: the house shelters daydreaming,
the house protects the dreamer,
the house allows one to dream in peace.

—*Gaston Bachelard*

Unscheduled Maintenance

> Having a clue of thread given him by Ariadne . . .
> he slew the Minotaur.
> —*Plutarch*

One heave after another, plank
on plank three-by-three, the deck
prepares itself to be re-decked,
cures in the sun on one yard end
as it dries in its rot on the other.
I suspect that once restored a house,
like the ship of Theseus, disputes
being called the identical house.
The hail pitted the roof to hell—
a pleasing sort of totaled;
dented up the bent-up
gutters which doomed to end
their pitiful, lackadaisical service.
New paint sits mixed in pails.
Plus the car—its black hood marked
with shimmering pocks
of swilling sky—and my kingdom
is adjusted at replacement cost.

Some say Ariadne, abandoned
by Theseus, hanged herself. Plutarch says
on his return from Crete, Theseus
put in at Delos and dedicated
to the temple there an image of Venus
Ariadne had given him,
and danced a dance preserved
to this day among the locals
formed of measured, dithyrambic

turnings and twistings, harkening back
to the winding dark returnings
of the labyrinth.

The baby's policy comes in force
today, his actuarial nest egg,
ab ovo. The yellow coreopsis
rabbits nibble down.
Squirrels chase tree to tree
across a scrubby lawn, their risks
diminished with dogs inside;
wife's clothes hang on the line.
An illicit memory importunes
my attention: woman
stripped in dry, tall grass;
warm February sun on the last day
for hunting quail; swollen
brown tick on my naked leg—

I cross myself with a hammer.

The war tilts on. A wind picks up.
Mills in the court of our kitchen garden
forgiveness that won't forget.
Good shepherds delight to count
by twos, I hear, and keep enclosures
well repaired, on budget.

The Exalted Shall Be Humbled

It came with the house, like the windows' dressings
or porch's swing, without negotiation, unlisted

as a feature. The structures must embellish the trees, if real
estate is what it means, but either way we became each other's.

That pronoun's antecedent is a discoid John Deere
outdoor thermometer affixed to the old box elder, and

I abhor it with God's hate for witnesses false and tawdry.

From my desk I confront its feckless sense of measure, give
or take ten degrees, and its blanched piss-green splash

of tractor kitsch. I imagine its leaping stag,
like the winging-bird stickers on the picture window,

driving off wildlife even as it forsakes good taste
for safety's sake. Explains a lot:

the backyard as a kind of fatal light mistaken for a getaway.

As the *Acer negundo* cannot shed it, the years having married
bark and plastic, they share a common joint, flesh of flesh.

Every time I ready to sunder them, some creeping kinship
halts me, groks us to détente. That bent gray needle

does its job well enough for who it's for; the tree keeps
throwing shade. The toolbox takes its hammer back

with cold regard and the meek go on inheriting.

Home After a Monthlong Job

we find the knee-high, non-compliant grass
cited by the city's code enforcer;
a mouse, dead and rotting, protests
where it fell in the center of the family room floor,
unalienated at last to its own environs.

Beneath my office window,
nested in a hollowed-out cubby beneath the sage,
newborn rabbit kits buck and writhe
like a bucket of worms, or the snakes in the hair of the Furies.

They are cold, hungry and orphaned to history.

Goaded by their squeals, I check
my spade is at hand, brace for the inevitable:
where some see cute and inchoate,
I see limp and delicate carcasses needing scooped
and tipped into a plastic grocery sack
before the dogs can devour them.
Later I read on Wikipedia that a rabbit doe
will often abandon her babies by day
but visit the litter each night for feeding, providing
of course she herself does not eat them.

On the half-dismantled unscreened porch
I'm fixing to rebuild and rescreen,
all along the oak joists I plug bullet-shaped wads of steel wool
into the perfect gallery holes
tunneled by carpenter bees now pissed,
embittered and disbelieving.

By revealing the hidden truth of our relation,
I will teach them the tragedy
of their fixed ideas,
what socially constructed nature is.

Object Permanence

Into the maple's hollow leader branch
a blur of black bird disappears;
how had I missed that large round hole,
or the industrious worry over many
days it obviously required?
I didn't think the tree that dead.
My ladder will not reach the spot
so for an hour I wait, curious what creature
I now will spare by sparing the tree,
slated as it is, was, for felling.

A boat-tailed grackle guards the margins,
swings and limns the perimeter
circuiting elm-to-shed, sycamore-to-wire-fence,
making flashy show of its crackling
caw and blue shook-foil head.

In the meantime I think about those
who walk great distances
wearing insufficient shoes; I ache
for those who ache under
the pretense that pathos is meiotic;
I say a prayer for poets
and the poems they will write,
for my next one, that there will be a next one—
but to speak of it will jinx it, so
I resign myself to sitting there,
one eye on the hole in my dying tree,
one eye marking the house's shadow creep
across the yard. What's a poem
for, anyway, if not to make the empty
spaces habitable?

A speckled starling emerges—
of the grackle nothing more is seen.

On This Day in 1805

Considerable rain. The Corps of Discovery is drenched, beached, miserable at the mouth of the Columbia, with nothing to do but think of hot food and the long trip back while watching porpoises and sea otters, seagulls and ducks. Meanwhile, my dad keeps seeing his dead cat in the window, content with its head still intact, as if the car that killed it were the phantom. Ten miles away, influenced by the Corps of Engineers, the Big Muddy ambles but no longer meanders. Strait jacketed. The day is bright and sunny, and thanks to last night's frost the redbud and box elder drop their leaves in a steady drizzle. We—the dogs and I—are housebound and happy, sleeping and reading Edward Abbey (respectively) here on Lot Eight (8) of T. N. Coats Subdivision of Part of Lot Forty-five (45) of Garth's Subdivision of Garth's Addition to the City of Columbia, Boone County, Missouri. No persons of note born or died.

Creamline

If there's a kindness
similar to milk,
it better be the raw kind,
pulled straight from
a vein-throbbed
taut and bloated udder,
nutrients intact,
illegal to sell
unless, like us,
you have anarchist
greengrocers who keep
a local-food shop,
where it's kept,
when available,
in the dairy case
in unmarked bottles.

So that I may hope,
do good and
dwell on the earth—
the sole demands,
if boiled down,
the galactic
grammatic I Am
saw fit to impose—
give me this brand
of beefy care,
grass-fed preferred.
But if I must settle,
as most often
I must, I'll take it

pasteurized but
unhomogenized:
heated and fortified
as legislated
but left in need
of shaking.

Why Should a Man Die While Sage Grows in His Garden?

Somewhere, maybe, there's ambition
to be a sleeper, to lag
in the high grass,
to slowly awaken, for a spell,
before inevitably drifting off again.
Somewhere a church
contains the true body of belief
and believes in nothing
but the certainty
of living while alive
and the holiness of what's imagined
regardless of the heart
and its disposition,
unfathomable and probably despicable anyway.
There, a man will be free
to seek the grounds of his own accusal,
to spurn or ignore
what gainsays his gutculture, lacks
truck with stomach, blood, brain and tongue—
whatever reckons itself
as one more senseless image of devotion.

As they must in every heaven-version,
Tibetan monks convene to work,
patient and sure
near a table of prayer wheels for sale,
constructing a mandala out of colored sands.
This contraption, in the vernacular
a *Garbhadhatu*—
part pretty cosmogram, part
theatrical revenue- and awareness-raiser—

maybe it is what they avow
it is: a fragile gate
that opens on a country of nowhere,
where symbols are real and the symbolized shadows.
Maybe the Buddha's spectacular release
is just a showy way of proposing that wholeness
of the self is plausible.

So yeah, if a site of instruction
exists where the God-object is a property
of this slow going (breathing
exercises optional),
then that's where I'll sign a mortgage
and mean a death pledge.
Weeds might overrule the beds long
before the note matures,
but that objection itself sustains
why a man might die while sage grows in his garden.

Nocturne, Past Midnight, Christmas Day

The dishwasher swells and whirrs, murmurs
        and groans and from here—
                to a mind made large by single malt,
            growing colder and
                in a mood for symbols—
I tremor at the commotion, as if a squall
                of wind and rain
    were lashing our country house door:
                despite the street lights blind-occluded,
                    curse the asbestos siding.

So in my rendition of a night song,
            the black Lab, asleep,
                must stand for nightingale,
    just as the scruffy tree she nests beneath
            must indicate giant fir.
                Scratch that. She watches, waits
out with me the struggling fire,
            all of us gathered
                    for a heat to catch
    we know is lost.
            It's late, half moon at best,
                    the woodbin empty.

This is not our parents' life.
        Though hardly our own
                at times, the logs were split
            with my father's axe;
                    this ring, repurposed,
    the one he and my mother
                bought and later stored.

What do we claim we think we want the most,
      that insoluble solid, like money but not quite—?

Nothing purchased, nothing redeemed.
                         The owl that flew at dusk
    has simply returned
        with its belly full.

If only it were so simple
    to implant, to bestow, to endow—

I would wrap and regift to you what is lost.

Clearly, my special pleading
      bears little semblance to the animal spirits
        that made this mess.
But count me shovel-ready—
    I won't be unsettled;
        here the tattered blankets,
    here the cave.

Ode to Dogwood Winter

Too soon up attic, the space heater has come down.
The last of the maul-split wood—twice-covered to cure over
　　summer—is back indoors.
Yet the grass needs cut.
Yet the garden needs opened and taxes still to do.
The dogs will not rouse to protect us from the mail.

The newborn sage, lately unfurled now turning blue will
　　undoubtedly rejuvenate.
Still, it's not enough to say, as young wives do who awaken to
　　themselves: it's hard but it's okay.

In my phantastic vision as the proto-husband, I aspire
　　to save them all.
Every earthbound woman, delivered from heavenly curses
　　and manly neglect, would know perfect solace and regular,
　　exhaustive satisfaction—plus all the yard work done.

One good end from this foul turn is that the stench of rotting
　　flowers, which follows, always, the week of glory-ridden
　　blossoms, has been stanched.
More snow is on the way.
Thanks to radar a sky need not turn gray to signal heavy weather.

Resolution

In the interest of economy—
      meant as thrift,
  meant as household management,
meant as *oikonomeia*: the basis of mercy, judgment
and degree
      weighed against circumstance and the frailty
that souls possess (or do not)
      —I pledge
to repair my pace and rhythms,
to fix my bond with time.
     I am in the measure of an hour poor.

On the ancient Chinese calendar, even today, a year
marks its passing by the New Moon
  preceding the onset of spring, called *Li Chun*.
    From the Waking of Insects,
through the Slight and Great Heats to its Limits
  just before the White Dew
    and the Solstice Colds, the year moves as it always has:
     by concept more than math,
image more than chart.

Can't we, can't you and I, do a little better, and let the pain of
  others be our guide?
Take the story of Li Yian, for example.
The matchmaker chose her husband, a civil servant of average
  mettle, for his skill with the abacus and his intimate
  knowledge of *bowu*: poetic curiosities like how many beads
  Li Po wore in his hair or the metaphorical correspondence
  between the cricket and the feminine ideal. She couldn't
  be blamed, though, for how strapped he kept the family

buying books. They loved retiring to the Abode of Fancy,
as they called their tea hut, where one would recite a
passage, then the other, then they'd compete to see who
came closest, to the page, to naming the other's source.
The winner drank the first cup of tea, that liquid jade.

We should imagine Li Yian here at her happiest.
As wars set on,
    from the north and then the west,
they were forced to divide the collection,
  selling, then relinquishing,
     and finally watching as an invading general
inherited a fine library.
Then her husband became her ancestor.
Then she lived unconsolably
       with another man
       with but two or three partial
books to remind her to believe that it had been real.

So if there's hope for me, let it come.

Courtesy's not yet demanded
  I say I pawned my best suit to buy wine for dinner,
  nor custom called me to excuse
    a pressing flight from barbarian hordes
by contending my mother has died.
  But I do tell myself other small, helpful lies.
Some mornings, even today, I truly believe the day
will not end if only I live rightly.
      At other times, like when I cannot find
  my keys, I tell myself I'd rather be
dead and kind of mean it.

A life can take us hours as sure as lines, and as
        sure as days are gods
        —history shows—
                    a house mismanaged falls.
        Where *jing ji*, less the art than science of exchange,
does not exist by instinct
                        it must, like meter, be added on.
If she'd forethought the Mongols' coming,
        if she'd possessed some lovestone capable
of forecasting when
                (and when not)
                    the Great Snows would block
the mountain passes,
        when the Pure Brightness would return to melt them
open,
would she have sewn those velvet pouches,
                or affixed them with silver pins and ceremony,
                for their most precious books?

Nature wins when nature's overcome.

This Poem Is Carbon Neutral

Across the street they think
we're eco-Kool-Aid drinkers: we sort glass and plastics
into blue bags, organics into clear ones, stuff
paper into paper sacks then treat
everything else like garbage.

But he thinks I'm a good neighbor,
and since we mend no fences I stop short of thinking
he's like Frost's old-stone savage
despite the Pall Malls
billowing with grandkids in the backseat,
windows up, despite the herbicide
and fungicide and fertilizer
liberally broadcast fall and spring. We wave
and shout news across the way though I suspect
he's deaf.

Otherwise our lifeworlds
barely intersect, our privacies mutually assured
except for now and again
when an egg is borrowed, or if the wind litters
his greensward with my recycling—
a magazine blow-in card or a pitched draft
or a crumpled receipt.
Once they walked across to inspect
then carried back a worn-out bookshelf we'd discarded.

Now and again I pop their cat
with a pellet gun to chase him off our feeders.

But when the trash trucks come
each Monday,
doing their slow-maw grinding action-non-action thing
and one truck stops for him
and one truck stops for me, we offset,
we reset, we're zero-sum.

Separated from His Natural Condition
by Tools of His Own Making

> Human beings exhibit an inborn tendency to carelessness,
> irregularity and unreliability in their work.
> —*Sigmund Freud*

My poet friend talks up her new novel
                                to the radio host as I,
            hard on my knees and cursing,
                        mismeasure and cut, glue, hammer, caulk and paint
                                this flimsy Brazil-milled trim,
            annoyed
                        with the typically shoddy
            state of thingcraft, by sacrifice
                                and my own long-tailed faith in chaos.

            This Sunday's Typika in the now three-season room
                        —chilly September breeze,
                                a companion choir of ranging flies—
            we meditate on cold facts
        that pass for self-knowledge:
                        my sole tradable skill is keeping a wet edge;
                nothing joins; the door slides on the hinge;
                        no line is sharp, no angle straight.
                                        I am too translatable.

Though I've terrorized
                to death the carpenter bees,
                                their nests shot full of liquid nails
                to order this porch for habitation,
                                still, I'm relying on distracted gazes
                to miss or only cooly notice

my constant
to-the-point-of-patterned imperfections.

What have I done, I have to wonder,
to have squandered my twice-born life
on the filling of gap after gap,
concealing the truth with silicone,
to have so reduced and lost
an irretrievable morning
to this—however crucial—finish work?
Even if I dwelling-build
for the sake of almighty love,
for the comfort and use of those I love
as I tell myself I do,
no matter how handy I prove, my unfitness
for the labor grates at the innate
sources of patience, unmakes
them to the verge of revolt. If the interviewer turned
and asked me
—how has householding changed your writing?—
I would say we are helped, by and large,
my writing and I, but sometimes
we'd rather be burning.

CHAPTER 4

IN WHICH *they seek the measure of art and love*

A man must keep within his compass.

—*Gawain Poet*

My Initiation Into Poetry

So I'm sitting out back, drinking a microbrew the neighbor gave me
that finishes on a rich almondy note with hints of chocolate and smoke,
swatting mosquitoes out for a blood meal but looking forward to dinner.
The open shed—half catastrophe, half ransacked labyrinth—taunts me,
dares me to configure and keep it as if I lived here. The baby toddles under
the sheets hanging from the line, lets out a cackling laugh, turns and does
it again. He stops, points and says "Caca! Caca!" as the dog pulls in its
haunches and with a furtive look of shame begins to shit. This is my life,
I realize as though it were a revelation, a still moment similar to one I
once had on a similar October day kneading manured loam and planting
pansies, which it surprises a lot of people to learn have antifreeze in their
veins and thrive in winter. Then, without any further prelude, I see this
vision of the Naked King crucified to the lopped oak, and watch the
dancers, red-eyed from the acrid smoke of the sacrificial fires, stamping
out the measures of the dance, their bodies bent uncouthly forward, with
a monotonous chant of "Kill! Kill! Kill!" and "Blood! Blood! Blood!"

He Leads the Way for His Sons to Follow

This is how I
move
through scenery
watch
him sway honeysuckle
snapped
against clapboard siding
chained
by the neighbor habit
flung
a blast leaving no one
dead
thank God thrown
clear
but not clearly

Year: Two

Nature is garrulous to the point of confusion;
let the artist be taciturn.
—*Paul Klee*

The hole is backfilled,

and the placenta

safely recycled beneath

the dense root ball of

the *Corylus avellena,*

what we call a contorted

filbert but goes by

other names: corkscrew

hazelnut, Harry

Lauder's Walking Stick,

or just plain old

Contorta. The label

tags it "winter interest"

because its gnarled limbs

will be

gaudiest bare.

Passersby rubberneck

already, and cars slowly veer

to get a closer look

even before the leaves

have dried and fallen.

You're sacked out

atop the covers, as is

your daylight rule.

Sometimes I jolt—

a flinty ache

that stabs me awake—

                                        to the baby's life:
                              alarmed to know he is
                              but not know
                                                    where he is. He is
with you, asleep.
                        As if it were
true that we're one
                                                    flesh, as I dug
                        that hole I marveled
                                    at how at ease I am
                        with our small circle.
It must be the curse
            of Adam that drives
                                          a man to circumvent,
                  with a metaphysical
                                    dread he calls honesty,
                        acts that mark
                  embodied confines
      between what is his
                                          and all that lies
                                    outside that sphere.
            In the legend of Eden,
                        limitlessness defines
                        the serpent's idea
of housekeeping. But
                                    to love—if I dare
                                    to call what I do that—
                  means to have ranks
                        to draw in, with
                                    margins to defend.

                  That tree's a shrub,
a misshapen English hedge

                                          they sculpt into a tree
by grafting. We thought
                        it was Oriental (blame
                                        our ignorance on
                                          once-lauded Harry's
                        now-dwindled fame),
                                but it's merely an ornamental
named for a balladeer.
You cough and Jonah
                        moans and, as I picture it,
                                        writhes beside you.
                                I trust your lungs are
                less blighted than they sound:
                                        just the residues
        of lodged pollen
                                and that snaky virus
                cluttering your hollows.
                It seems to catch him,
                                        but then you both
                drift back to sleeping
                                        out of sinuous habit, as
                                the cut-back twists
                of ivy and the running
tillers of cleared Bermuda
                        will reinvade my stone-
                                ringed bed. The quirky
                                        avellena, whose drooping
                                fertile catkins we may move
                                        before we see,
                        will survive us, I hope; future
                owners will never know
        the joy it fed on. Not
        that anyone would care; it's our

anniversary and placentas

are grotesque. Since so few

believe in myths

or the power of the ground

to summon creatures

sewn with dragon's teeth,

or see in the Milky Way

a spinning Ouroboros

or the names of fated lovers—

it's safe to say they won't

come round very soon

before our spin on the gyre

ends. The miracle

is that's okay, and so

if we stroll beneath the stars—

Roamin' in the Gloamin'

as Harry Lauder sang it—

and I find you bonnie and you

find me brave, we'll find

nothing strange or fearful

in being swallowed

by what already has us.

Early Retirement

It's an experiment doomed
before it begins,
grounded as it is in nothing more sure
than this draft of thought,
but what if we ditched
our hope in hereafters, wrote it off
as one more worldly expense,
and like a sacked Rome or toppled Colossus
let whatever everlasting is
—or what promise our portfolio holds—
babble and overrun us?

Once we reach the end
of our rutted dirt road, the one
that wends to a grassy tract
some relative bought and then forgot,
and squat in the trailer
we've reclaimed from the prairie—
the rest is fieldwork.
Forced to make a hard and habit-
forming peace with the bluestem and millet,
the switchgrass and grama,
we'll test by rote
the suspect theory that the kosmos
vibrates at the feet of Kansas.

Let's bring the pups,
but leave behind our previous attempts
at ill-conceived revisions;
let's be satisfied with what the land
provides and learn to trust

our faith in art and the body's selection.
Let the earth supply its instructors.

Outside at night, locusts will sing
along with crickets and whippoorwills,
and bats will swing down from hidden roosts
to eat the moths who tell themselves
(or believe at least)
our single homely light
strung-wired to the engine is the moon.
Those scattered wings beneath
it fall because the bats
just eat the middles:
our children will be their students.

When in October the hunters come
who've used this place
as cabin and blind for years,
they'll meet a woman's welcome to beat
the stand—hot brown
drinks aplenty—and a knowing
nod at the composting john;
the dogs will play
with their business-minded hounds.
And while I regale them
with stories of the city,
true tales packed with stalking and the kill,
ferocious beasts and heroic o'erleaping,
you can help the deer escape,
down cellar or across the back pasture.

Wouldn't it be sweet then,
if amidst those browning grasses,
within our little plot
(even as our stocks compounded nicely),
if we became—
as nature and the ancients
kind of hint for those who'd strive
to use the world without a show of force—
saints of sorts:
fading into gold that fades to white.

These Late Eclipses in the Sun and Moon Portend No Good to Us

We rejoice at what we forgot
to schedule to witness,
however glad we
are for what occurred,
secure (and maybe too secure)
events no longer need us
to see them to make
a deep and well-deserved
impression. Next time
the lawn chairs; next time keep
the kids awake; next time
undertake the *askesis*
of description.
This time we sit in a restaurant,
stare at menus, eat
in silence as outside an older
fight ensues: the dragon
of the end of the world devours
its own ever-brooding egg.
We think penumbral shadows
tack and slide and fade
into deeper umbral shades;
yellow-whites give way
to yellow-grays, which fade
to copper-cratered
hazy reds. We think wrong.

Cafe Rotavirus

Last time we all
ate here, a Sunday, after
the baby played with
—chewed on—
their toys: six
days and nights
of puke and diarrhea.
This stuff kills
starving kids in Africa,
underdeveloped as
electrolyte industries
are there.

But I cannot stop
returning and returning.
What pathogenesis
makes me weak
for, so consoled by,
this biscuits-and-gravy—
though I cannot
stop imagining
trillions of rotifer-driven
microbes racing
around this apparent
locus amoenus
like, but not like,
animated soap
bubbles scrubbing up
bathtub scum?

To believe in history,
now that fixed
stars are not so fixed,
might be to believe
each instant struggles—
fatally, hopefully—
to loose itself from
some unoriginate whole.
But (and this makes
instinctual sense
so long as instinct is
but undigested
experience) it may also,
or maybe instead
be the collective orgy
clearing its gorge,
suffusing each instant
with the particles
of every other
but in tastier order,
because nothing is real
until it means,
and nothing means
until it returns,
returns like a dog returns,
as it will with verve
to a baby's vomit.

my last fetus

like you, I'll keep it brief

we feel: anger sick despair numb relief
in no right order

vexed to learn that nothing soothes
nothing can be said
that zeroes out in consolation

your brother hurtles along his way
oblivious
but it's not personal

we go about ours, as the living must,
and obviously it is

I sense you among the patient choir
of the unborn
where the aborted, the miscarried, the cessated ectopics,
the test-tubed and petri-dished
gather but are bored

who would happily trade that cloud kingdom
of grace and equanimity
for a taste of workaday desperation
who swear they would be grateful for every seizure and spasm

sorry, I really am,
things didn't pan out
chromosomally

she has named you
clementine

Stray Paragraphs, February, Year of the Rat

Why we resist coming after, coming second, coming late
        but not last
    I cannot say, but we seem to, though we should root to, if we
            had the sense of a brush pile, or the squirrels.

There are no gifts that are not dowries; etymons and archaeologies
    like that first divorce, the division of day from night—
        precursor to the watershed, the neighborhood's
    downward contours—that prototype fracture
            which still defines
                    where runoffs deposit their wrack lines.

What accumulates is not a reason, not debris but tablature,
                adagia, apologia, full stops and half lives along with
    twigs and trash,
            notations scratched out with unremarkable style.
We have commissioned a longitudinal study, so give it time,

but try to avoid that ur-emphasis poets put on being,
where what is best left unaccented they prod into becoming
        something else,
                a thing at all, that wants nothing anyway, more or less.
Just like our lost baby, our would-be who would-not-be,
    who will miss the seventh moon's scheduled swell
            but asks for no condolence.

February, old rite-monger, this is how you will be welcomed:
    in the name of those who won't be.

The firstborn pries up a corner
                of the living room rug,

disinters the filthy tape, the wood floor's bright parts,
          and nothing else
     the naked eye can see, however suggestive the figure.
Even so it ties the place together
   in a way you, middle sister, might have
       but, bereft of origin will only, with us,
      await recombination, some saving throw, mitochondrial.

My son, two, who wakes in our bed and screams in terror if we're not there because he thinks we have betrayed and/or abandoned him,

        used to stoke pity, even fear,
        in places where now I am merely spent.

        Now he prods me, in the poking sense,
        to what I must have known but had forgotten:
        sleep—putting oneself to
                and putting oneself back to—
        is no more natural (i.e. inevitable)
                than a rockslide or avalanche.
        Though once the accident
        is triggered
        and tidal event is made,
        there's only negation—and what follows—
            or acceptance:
        to inwardly absorb the blows an environment imposes.

        This is the faith of indulgent fathers.
        This is the faith of the family bed.
        This is the faith that attachment is not a thing
            to be dissolved,
                that suffering has its end
        in something other than ending.

        While lying in the dark, waiting for his breathing
        to slow and grip to loosen, signs
        that it's safe to edge to the edge of the bed and maybe, maybe,
            slip out and live a little,
        finish a film or book or write or make love to my wife
        as I hear normal adults do of an evening,

I wonder (or possibly dream) if van Gogh faced
        this same dreadful pause—
perhaps he's washing potatoes,
                or he's sprawled atop his straw mattress
touching himself with fingers
caked in pigment, lead- and arsenic-laced—
        each time a new self-portrait
                imagined itself, begged to be attempted,
prodding him, in the goading sense,
        to resist the warmth of the work's opposite,
that emerald quiver at the margin
of a chasm
of an oblivion ceaselessly beckoning, drawing
        a man back to fall into it and rest.

He must get up, he must get up
                and paint it before it engulfs him.

Clean Me

I love to watch these bodies, so lovely and so shapely,

each a proxy (or is it metonymy) for the other.

It's almost as if Eros himself came down and fashioned

them out of his nearly perfect experience

—and in a small town in the middle of Missouri no less—

so smartly draped and about their business they are

as if it were Paris or Milan or New York

and life, so meaningful, without boredom, want, or iniquity.

Although my work is urgent, I attend to them

with care, as if my attention could be exchanged for their secrets

to a more phenomenal life, to unembittered carnality.

Could the solution be that simple,

could the mere act of shaping an appearance

out of fabric, talk, and the incoherent dust of daily rounds

qualify us, render us worthy for affection?

We no longer believe in child gods—and really why should we?—

yet up and down the street, parked cars mock me

with these letters, traced in filth, crying out for action.

The Banging Wall

Sea Lion Inn, Netarts, Oregon Coast

On the cosmic-lodestone level of my encompassed soul,
              that region which by ferromagnetism locates
      the most attractive person in any room
                 or detects in telltale traffic shifts
the proximity of a Starbucks or Taco Bell,
                  I must have understood the smirky glance
           of our barrel-chested motel neighbor—
                     cast at me and then my son
      as we passed his open door
               along the upper breezeway—
to be a kind of troth, an earnest
              upon the performance to be played later.

Which is why it feels so ordinary, just as our lights turn out
          —holy family arrayed in queen size, child between—
      just as I invoke our habitual nightly prayer
in which we recover from forgetting
              some particular goods of the day, we hear
         the achey moans of fore-pleasure,
              then low grunts and bedsqueaks.
Jennifer says, "I thought this only happened in movies"
        and, as if on cue, their headboard bangs our common wall.

Jonah lies still, unimpressed or too fatigued to stir.
      It's clear no petitions are in the offing.
              But fasting is its own peculiar kind of plea
   —and sleepy but the body
            craving images—
         so our silent but hardly quiet vigil
becomes the kind of witness

that longs expectantly for future bliss,
that argues, as Julian's showings did,
that every kind of suffering is the suffering of labor,
and every conception an exploding star.
So in the void of Our-Fathers,
of kingdom-comes and thy-will-be-dones,
the angels stop upon their ladders
and we gather to listen around the noise of love's
most native deed, their thwack-thwacking,
and submit ourselves to this trespass.

Earlier that day, I'd hiked to the summit of Cape Falcon,
kid strapped to my back, and while he, once freed,
ran in and out of the tall sedge,
I perched cliffside
as a flotilla of wave-desperate surfers
drifted toward shore 800 feet below.
Somewhere down on the beach my pregnant wife
read *O Pioneers!* and
awaited our descent.
Atop that promontory,
on the wild verge of America,
a better man might have better clung to the elements
so as to wring out of them some real clarification,
might have relearned how to look at the world
(which of course is what Oregon's for).
My attempt to imitate the conditions of solitude
ended abruptly to chase down a feral boy oblivious
to danger or death, on whose behalf I am regularly forced
to keep my being in disrepair.
As we started back down the trail,
my vain wish for a minute or two of nonduality
reminded me of a time in grad school when,

sick of my thesis on mystical speech,

               I laid my head on the keyboard, fell asleep

and, as if lifted into space à la Kepler's Dream,

                 beyond Augustine's cloud and tongue of time,

      I saw (well, *beheld* I guess)

                     the helixed and hyaline ribbon

        that sometimes stands for ALL THAT IS

           lengthen out before and behind me.

                        I sought my place along it—

          which seemed the thing to do—

when the voice of the vision said without saying:

               you can not know for whom you work.

The next door thunk-thunk-

                   thunking builds toward crescendo,

        and while scientists somewhere fret

           over plummeting sperm counts and prana,

   I am content to attend

      —solemnly, as our bemused role in this petty worship entails—

             and to praise the witchery of sense

      that inscribes a circumference for every center,

what a god requires to yearn itself into a zygote.

      With a concluding boom our neighbors attain

                their singularity,

    an event Hindu rishis call the Provision of Images,

when a seer becomes the thing seen.

        The energy of the place approaches rest;

           we drift toward sleep on hard pillows

    beneath the emptied ladders.

We Do Whatever You Ask and Say

Begin with something, anything
crenellated, notched,
a built-in place for gunners
to stand and a place
for them to hide.
We forget the cannon
is not a kind of gun
but the essence of gun—
since we believe,
as biology teaches,
things progress
simpler to complex—
invented by angels to kill
angels and given its name not
by Milton—who called it
a pillar on wheels, imagined it
belching from its hellish
glut Thunderbolts and Hail
Of Iron Globes—
but by some rank Viking
who named his war
engine after his woman,
Gunhilda, to enflame
with longing
his lonely job of
disemboweling the enemy
with fiery projectiles.
Far from home
but in the name of home.

Live and Find Out Who You Are

When the drain clogged
and the cleanout
burst and chard-scrap water
flooded our dank
underbelly of a crawlspace,
the house soon smelt
of decaying organic
matter as if we lived, as it felt,
in a molding dishrag atop
a sopping foundation

but as I, a good soldier,
low-crawled across that slimy
trench to interrogate
the erupted pipe,
a corroded iron line
unsweatable as indispensable
drip-dripping
into our mephitic
tarn with the restraint
of a dominatrix
at one with technique,
I accepted as true,
all at once and without fear,
the noble lie
of my birth and was—
immersed in a filth of my own
contriving, indicted
for a failure to compost
my waste, this mud
as my mother—born anew.

COLOPHON

This book is typeset in Dante, a font designed by Giovanni Mardersteig and Charles Malin for Monotype and initially used in a 1955 edition of Boccaccio's *Life of Dante*. Titles are set in Mercury Text, and the cover title in Knockout, both produced by the foundry of Hoefler & Frere-Jones.

ABOUT THE AUTHOR

John Estes directs the Creative Writing Program at Malone University in Canton, Ohio, where he lives with his wife and sons.

in memoriam Irvin Ray Estes, 1934-2010